ETHICS

BULLET GUIDE

D0813350

Hodder Education, 338 Euston Road, London NW1 3BH

Hodder Education is an Hachette UK company

First published in UK 2011 by Hodder Education

This edition published 2011

Copyright © 2011 Robert Anderson

The moral rights of the author have been asserted

Database right Hodder Education (makers)

Artworks (internal and cover): Peter Lubach

Cover concept design: Two Associates

British Library Cataloguing in Publication Data: a catalogue record for this title is available from the British Library.

10 9 8 7 6 5 4 3 2 1

The publisher has used its best endeavours to ensure that any website addresses referred to in this book are correct and active at the time of going to press. However, the publisher and the author have no responsibility for the websites and can make no guarantee that a site will remain live or that the content will remain relevant, decent or appropriate.

The publisher has made every effort to mark as such all words which it believes to be trademarks. The publisher should also like to make it clear that the presence of a word in the book, whether marked or unmarked, in no way affects its legal status as a trademark.

Every reasonable effort has been made by the publisher to trace the copyright holders of material in this book. Any errors or omissions should be notified in writing to the publisher, who will endeavour to rectify the situation for any reprints and future editions.

Hachette UK's policy is to use papers that are natural, renewable and recyclable products and made from wood grown in sustainable forests. The logging and manufacturing processes are expected to conform to the environmental regulations of the country of origin.

www.hoddereducation.co.uk

Typeset by Stephen Rowling/Springworks

Printed in Spain

Dedicated to the memory of Ralph,
the best of dogs and the sweetest of friends

About the author

Robert Anderson is a freelance teacher, writer, editor and translator. He studied Modern Languages at the University of Exeter and went on to live in France for a number of years.

He has taught in schools in France and the United Kingdom and has worked in educational publishing for more than a decade. He has published a wide variety of children's and adult books, including a series of books on design icons for London's Design Museum as well as online courses for the Tate Gallery.

Acknowledgements

I would like to thank everyone at Hodder – especially Sam Richardson, Helen Rogers and Laura Davis – for their support (and patience!) during the writing of this book. My thanks also to David Porteous, David Price and Peter Lubach, editor, proofreader and illustrator respectively.

Robert Anderson, Scott Cottage, Roxburghshire
May 2011

Contents

Introduction

Ethics is perhaps the one branch of **philosophy** that has a direct impact on our everyday lives:

* In our **personal** lives we may sometimes wonder what to do 'for the best'? Should we tell someone a relationship is over now, rather than letting it simply fade away? Should we inform on a friend whom we know is drink-driving, putting himself and others at risk?
* In our **professional** lives, too, we may face even more dramatic dilemmas: a doctor, managing scarce resources, may have to decide to which patient he or she will offer a liver transplant (the young alcoholic or the elderly teetotaller?); a soldier must choose whether to shoot a teenage boy who is about to throw a grenade.
* On a **political** level, a government may have to decide whether it is right to go to war; while citizens may have to justify their decision to rebel against their leaders.

As this rapid overview suggests, ethics is very often not about choosing between a right action and a wrong one (things are rarely that simple), but between two competing 'rights' or even between two 'wrongs'. For this reason – and because ethics places **responsibility** for our actions (and even for the **consequences** of those actions) squarely on our shoulders – making moral choices can be a perplexing, even terrifying affair.

Through the ages, moral philosophers have attempted to clarify the way we think about our dilemmas. They have tried to equip us with the moral **armour** we need to face up to our choices and to provide moral **road maps** to guide us through life's ethical minefields. In this short book, I aim to introduce you to the most important of their ideas and how they can be applied to everyday issues and choices.

1 What is ethics?

Understanding ethics

Ethics is a branch of philosophy that asks fundamental questions about **right and wrong**, good and bad. Such questions can include:

* **Which** acts are right? Which wrong?
* **How** do we decide what makes one act 'good' and another 'bad'?
* What **values** ought we to live by?
* What is the **extent** of our ethical duties – ourselves, our nearest and dearest, every one of our fellow human beings?
* What is the ultimate **goal** of making ethical choices?

Ethics is a branch of philosophy that asks fundamental questions about right and wrong

In this chapter we'll look a little more closely at what ethics might mean (and crucially what it *doesn't* mean) and how it relates to other human fields of activity and human capacities:

* the relationship between ethics and **religion**
* the role of **common sense** and **reason**
* the role of the **emotions**
* ethics as an active, 'non-closed' process and how it differs from **moralism**.

● 'What's the right thing to do?'

Ethics and religion

* Religions generally have a strong moral quality – they often provide believers with **ready-made rules**, telling them what it is right (good) and what it is wrong (evil) to do. The most obvious example is the Ten Commandments found in Judaism and Christianity.

* Religions also provide believers with a powerful **motivation** for acting well (on the religion's terms) – the believer will be ultimately rewarded for his or her obedience, for example, by being admitted to Heaven. Fear of punishment – the 'fire and brimstone' of Hell – is a further spur.

* Not all religions, it must be said, provide followers with moral 'commandments' or threaten them with draconian punishments. For example, Shinto – the ancient religion of Japan – does not concern itself with right and wrong, reward and punishment, in this sense.

Christianity, Judaism and Islam all teach that core moral rules come **directly** from God. For a secular ethicist, however, the notion of God-given rules leads to a kind of **ethical dead end**:

* God has ordered me to act in a certain way
* what He commands must be good and right
* goodness and rightness have no other meaning than what God commands.

Such a believer effectively gives up all his or her freedom to decide what is right and wrong, and the whole project of ethics is consequently undermined.

Morality without God

Believers often argue that without religion the individual loses his or her 'moral compass'. An atheist would argue the opposite: if we do not have divine commands, it is we alone who have responsibility for making ethical decisions, of determining what is right. It's in our hands, and so we're much more likely to make sure we get it right!

Common sense and reason

If we accept that it is we human beings who have responsibility for making our own moral rules, then how should we go about this? What inner resources can we turn to in order to work out what's good and what's bad?

* **Common sense** may be an obvious and not unreasonable answer, though exactly what constitutes common sense is open to debate. 'Plain good sense' tells us that it's wrong to kill another human being: experience tells us that it just leads to misery and probably more murders. And, anyway, 'everyone' agrees that murder is wrong, don't they?
* During the eighteenth century – a period known as the Enlightenment – many philosophers argued that **reason** was the best guide to making moral judgements. Reason is much more rigorous and solid than common sense – it is cool-headed and logical and, unlike common sense, scrupulously avoids subscribing to common opinion.

6

As we'll see, two of the most influential ethical theories practised today – utilitarianism and deontology – have their origins during this 'Age of Reason'.

Ethical relativism

The problem with such a rough-and-ready approach to ethics as common sense is that ethical values and norms can vary widely from culture to culture, as well as through time. While some wrongs such as murder and theft may be universally agreed upon, others – like homosexuality or sex before marriage – provoke widely differing **opinions**.

● Putting our decisions under moral scrutiny…

The moral sense

Do we really need to agonize over the rightness and wrongness of our actions? Do we need to submit them to the moral microscope of reason? Don't we in some sense instinctively **feel** when we are doing the right thing?

Some ethical philosophers have argued that we (or that most of us) do have such an innate capacity to tell right from wrong – a **moral sense** – just as we have an innate capacity to tell whether something is beautiful or not – an **aesthetic sense**. Our moral and aesthetic senses may, in some philosophical accounts, even be the same thing – what is good is beautiful and vice versa.

Our moral sense encompasses emotions and faculties such as pity, love and imagination. **Empathy** – the imaginative capacity to imagine yourself 'in another's shoes' – is key here.

Hume on the moral sense

The best-known philosophical proponent of the moral sense was the Scottish philosopher **David Hume** (1711–76). In *A Treatise of Human Nature*, he rejected outright the idea that reason (rational thought) can help us to make moral rules or act well:

* reason does not motivate us to do anything (it is 'inert', to use Hume's term), let alone make moral distinctions
* it is our emotions (or 'passions') that drive us towards good actions and away from bad ones.

The idea of a moral sense is profoundly **optimistic** – humans, in this view, are to a degree wired up to make good choices. Clearly, however, the concept has many limitations: how can we really trust our emotions? And what happens when our moral instincts are flatly contradicted by another person's?

An active process

I hope that from the preceding few pages you will have gathered that:

* ethics is a complex but deeply engaging subject
* it is not about **moralizing** – unthinkingly and intolerantly 'laying down the law' – but is an active, impassioned process of engagement with ourselves, others and the world
* ethical thinking involves both the **intellect** and the **emotions**; if we are to make choices with only either one or the other, we are likely to 'come a cropper'
* while we may well use ethical rules, values and theories to help us make the right choices, ethics is always an **open question**
* it's about being responsible and taking a risk.

In the rest of the book, we'll be looking at:

1 some key **ethical theories**, or ways of thinking, *and*
2 the **application** of these ideas to specific ethical problems and dilemmas.

These together constitute the two principal branches of ethics: **theoretical** and **applied**.

The following mind map may help you as you read through this book:

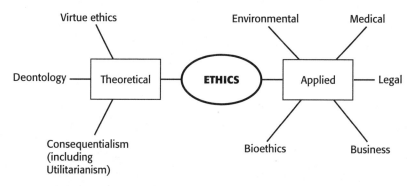

2 Virtue ethics

Ethical thinking

In this and the following two chapters we'll be looking at the **three main approaches** to ethical thinking:

1 **virtue ethics** – which stresses the importance of the character of the moral agent (the person making the ethical choice)

2 **consequentialism** – which sees the consequences of an act as being the best guide to its rightness or wrongness (**utilitarianism** is the 'classic' form of consequentialism and is what we will focus on here)

3 **deontology** – which gives pride of place to rules or duties.

Such approaches are not necessarily mutually exclusive.

Virtue ethics stresses the importance of the character of the agent

We'll begin with virtue ethics, as this was the approach typically taken by the ancient Greeks – the originators of the Western ethical tradition. Virtue ethics remained a powerful ethical yardstick until the eighteenth-century Enlightenment, when it was eclipsed by deontology and utilitarianism.

In this chapter, then, we will look at:

* what exactly is meant by 'virtue ethics'
* the ethical thought of **Aristotle**
* the concepts of *arete* and *eudaimonia*
* some modern virtue ethicists as well as some **key criticisms** of the approach.

Practice makes perfect

What makes an act good? The outcome? The rule followed? Or the goodness, or virtue, of the person who performs the act?

The ancient Greeks took the last view. A virtuous person does not necessarily make good choices of course, but he is more likely to do so. And he is good because he has acquired the skills and talents ('virtues') that are needed to make the right decisions. For example:

* he has learned to be **clear-sighted** and therefore has a better idea of the outcomes of his actions.
* over time he has steeled himself to be **courageous** enough to look at a situation square in the face and to face up to his responsibilities.

● The virtuous person is like an athlete who trains and practises hard so that when he does meet a challenge – the moral hurdle, so to speak – he overcomes it with panache!

Bullet Guide: Ethics

CASE STUDY: Three ethical approaches to cheating

Imagine someone has offered you a chance to see a question paper a couple of days before you go into an exam. You refuse (of course!) but on what grounds?

* The **deontologist** (as we'll see) would argue that, if everyone cheated, then there would be little point to the exam and that therefore they have a *duty* not to cheat.
* The **utilitarian** might argue that, while the cheater would of course benefit from cheating (a *small*, 'good' consequence), the exam system as a whole would be undermined (a *large*, bad consequence).
* The **virtue ethicist** would have developed the integrity not to be tempted to cheat at all; he or she will have had the good sense to have revised anyway and would have the courage and fortitude to face the exam unaided.

In a sense the virtue ethicist minimizes the moral dilemma in advance by sheer **strength of character**.

Aristotle

Earlier Greek philosophers – Socrates and Plato – had debated ethical ideas, but Plato's pupil **Aristotle** (384–322 BCE) was the first to devote extensive writings explicitly to the subject. Aristotle's two principal contributions to ethics are:

1 *Nicomachean Ethics*
2 *Eudemian Ethics*.

The first, in particular, exerted an enormous influence over the development of ethics for some two thousand years!

For Aristotle, ethics was pre-eminently a **practical** subject. It was about learning to live in the best possible way, realizing one's potential as a person, and thus contributing to the overall good of society.

18

The *Nicomachean Ethics* – named after Aristotle's son Nicomachus – is a surprisingly approachable and lively (if rather long) text. It is full of pithy, quotable statements, which perhaps in part explains the work's enduring popularity. Here are a few:

> To enjoy the things we ought and to hate the things we ought has the greatest bearing on excellence of character.

> We must as second best... take the least of the evils.

> One swallow does not make a summer, nor does one day; and so too one day, or a short time, does not make a man blessed and happy.

> It is well said, then, that it is by doing just acts that the just man is produced, and by doing temperate acts the temperate man; without doing these no one would have even a prospect of becoming good.

Arete and *eudaimonia*

Virtue is at the core of Aristotelian ethics. Aristotle's word is ***arete***, which properly means **'excellence'** (it was often used to describe the prowess of athletes). As we've seen, virtue is not something we're born with fully formed (being good by nature is no virtue at all) but is something we have to **practise hard** to develop (remember: 'one swallow does not make a summer').

Important examples of *arete* for Aristotle include:

* courage
* temperance
* generosity
* truthfulness
* friendliness.

It is only through perfecting these virtues (see the 'Golden Mean') that the individual can achieve ***eudaimonia*** – human flourishing or happiness – which Aristotle considered was the highest good and goal of philosophy.

The Golden Mean

Achieving any one of the virtues, for Aristotle, was like learning a difficult balancing trick between two undesirable extremes – **excess** and **deficiency**. For example, courage stood in the middle between recklessness and cowardice – learning to be courageous was a process of **tempering** natural propensities to either extreme.

Here is a table showing some more examples:

Excess	Virtue	Deficiency
Prodigality	Generosity	Meanness
Boastfulness	Truthfulness	False modesty
Self-indulgence	Temperance	Insensibility

This striving for the temperamental 'middle state' (as Aristotle called it) is often known as the **Golden Mean** and, in Greek thought, was closely associated with the pursuit of the 'beautiful'. (Think of all those beautiful classical Greek statues – neither too fat, nor too thin, showing neither too little, nor too much emotion! – embodiments of *eudaimonia*.)

Proponents and critics

It would be wrong to think that virtue ethics belongs to a dead and, for most of us, forgotten world. Its humane and humanist emphasis on the **individual** and what he or she can achieve, together with its ultimate concern with a flourishing **community**, makes it particularly inspirational in the contemporary world.

Some **modern ethical thinkers** who have sought to revive virtue ethics include:

Philippa Foot (1920–2010) who, in books such as *Virtues and Vices and Other Essays in Moral Philosophy* (1978), sought to 'update' Aristotelian ethics.	**Alasdair MacIntyre (1929–)** who, in *After Virtue* (1981), challenged Enlightenment ethical systems such as utilitarianism and argued for a return to virtue ethics.	**Martha Nussbaum (1947–)** who, in the *Fragility of Goodness* (1991), emphasized the importance of the individual's vulnerability as they struggle towards goodness.

Aristotelian virtue ethics, nonetheless, has attracted criticism. Objections include:

* Virtues are always **relative to the culture** that propounds them – Aristotle's virtues, for example, grew out of and reflected the aristocratic, male-dominated ethos of classical Athens; they were elitist then and are elitist now and have little relevance to today's society. (Of course, it is always possible for us to update what constitutes a virtue but that in itself can cause problems.)
* Virtues are of little use when it comes to **making laws**. We need to work out which *acts* are wrong; it's not enough for individuals to be left to decide what's right or wrong. The virtue ethicist would counter that our rulers should themselves be virtuous and therefore would make good laws.

● The virtuous person does not need to be told what is right and wrong…

3 Utilitarianism

Making moral choices

The ethical system known as **utilitarianism** puts human **wellbeing** at the very heart of moral choice making. Whatever action or moral code has the outcome of producing the most wellbeing for the most people is to be considered to be the greatest good. As such, it is a version of **consequentialism**.

Utilitarianism was – and continues to be – the dominant ethical system in the development of Western liberal democracy and values.

Utilitarianism puts human wellbeing at the very heart of moral choice making

● ●

'The greatest happiness of the greatest number is the foundation of morals and legislation.'

Jeremy Bentham

In this chapter we will look at:

* the origins of utilitarianism in the thought of Jeremy Bentham
* the nature of human happiness
* some problems associated with utilitarianism and some possible resolutions
* its influence.

Key term: utility

The term 'utilitarianism' derives, of course, from the word 'utility' – usefulness or functionality. For utilitarian ethicists, utility is a substitute for the usual terms applied to the goal of ethics – 'the good'.

Pain and pleasure

The concept of utilitarianism can seem so obvious that it can be a surprise to discover that it was only first systematically formulated in the eighteenth century – by the British lawyer and philosopher **Jeremy Bentham** (1748–1832).

Bentham wanted to put ethics (as well as many other things) on a clear, rational footing. At the beginning of his most famous work, *An Introduction to Principles of Morals and Legislation* (1789), he stated:

'The Nature has placed mankind under the governance of two sovereign masters, pain and pleasure. It is for them alone to point out what we ought to do, as well as to determine what we shall do.'

The happiness equation

To work out what we ought to do, we have 'only' to consider whether our actions are likely to increase the totality of pleasure and decrease the totality of pain. To do this, Bentham even came up with a calculation method, which he called the **hedonic** or **felicific calculus**.

The variables of this 'happiness equation' are shown in the chart below:

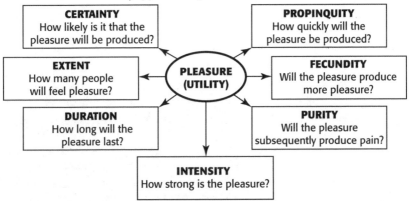

CERTAINTY
How likely is it that the pleasure will be produced?

PROPINQUITY
How quickly will the pleasure be produced?

EXTENT
How many people will feel pleasure?

PLEASURE (UTILITY)

FECUNDITY
Will the pleasure produce more pleasure?

DURATION
How long will the pleasure last?

PURITY
Will the pleasure subsequently produce pain?

INTENSITY
How strong is the pleasure?

What is human happiness?

Bentham's ideas proved enormously influential not only in philosophy and ethics but also socially and politically (see below). However, later utilitarian thinkers have usually been dissatisfied with Bentham's conception of human happiness (and hence the good) as a mere matter of pleasure and pain:

* Is human psychology, they have wondered, really as simple and as brutish as that?
* And what if the pleasure is itself a transparent wrong – the abuse of children, rape, or murder?

John Stuart Mill

The Victorian philosopher and politician John Stuart Mill (1806–73) argued that human beings can act, not only out of a desire for pleasure, but out of a sense of **duty**. Moreover, doing one's duty can itself produce happiness in the doer. This is an idea that might be summed up in a famous quote by the Roman writer Cicero: 'Virtue is its own reward.'

Henry Sidgwick

Another British moral philosopher, Henry Sidgwick (1838–1900), also sought to refine Bentham's concept of happiness. He stressed:

* the principle that 'the good of any one individual is of no more importance, from the point of view… of the Universe, than the good of any other'
* and that therefore every individual should strive to act in such a way as to maximize others' happiness or pleasure while not neglecting their own.

In this way Sidgwick sought to rescue utilitarianism from the charge of being merely a philosophical cover for individual **hedonism** or egoism.

To do good, we have to treat *everyone* equally – our nearest and dearest, the perfect stranger and even unknown persons on the other side of the planet.

Some tricky problems

As you have already discovered for yourself, there are some other major problems with utilitarianism as a guide to 'being good':

What would you do?

* Imagine a dictator is murdering his own people in order to hold on to power (this isn't hard). Would it be right – even our duty – to assassinate him in order to save the lives of many others?
* Bog-standard **utilitarianism** would answer with a resounding 'yes' – the pain suffered by the dictator would be a hundred times outweighed by the 'pleasure' of the countless number who would as a consequence survive. The end justifies the means.
* From a **common sense** point of view, however, an act of murder may make us feel queasy, ethically speaking – is murder ever right?

Some utilitarian thinkers have sought to remedy this problem by distinguishing between:

1 **act consequentialism** – which looks only at the positive consequences of any particular act
   and
2 **rule consequentialism** – which argues that we should follow a set of rules that we believe produces more positive consequences than any other set of rules.

In (1) the assassination of the dictator could be justified. In (2) the assassination would never be justified if the rules happened to include a prohibition on murder.

Other thinkers have argued for a more measured approach to utilitarianism. We live in the real world, which is chaotic and messy; we should, and can only, try to ensure that the consequences of our actions are **'good enough'**.

The influence of utilitarianism

Despite the philosophical problems associated with utilitarianism, its impact on the development of modern liberal values has been enormous. In its determination to sweep away irrational, hidebound moral codes and to replace them with an ethical system rooted in reason, wellbeing and equality, utilitarianism provided a **philosophical foundation** for social and political reforms such as:

* equal legal and political **rights for women** – both Bentham and Mill were ardent supporters of women's rights
* an end to **discrimination against homosexuals** – consensual sex never harms anyone!
* **prison reform** – Bentham argued that the primary goal of imprisonment should not be the punishment of criminals but their rehabilitation
* **animal rights** – Bentham (again!) was an early advocate of animal rights on the basis that animals, as sentient beings, feel pleasure and pain, too (see Chapter 8).

CASE STUDY: Women's rights

In *The Subjection of Women* John Stuart Mill wrote a passionate **utilitarian critique** of the position of women in Victorian society. Denied the right to vote and equal access to education, and generally subordinate to men, women were hindered from pursuing their own happiness. Moreover, in denying women equality, society as a whole failed to benefit from the talents and skills of one half of its citizens – from the utilitarian point of view a reckless waste of their potential utility.

● Utilitarianism provided an ethical foundation for late-Victorian feminism.

4 Deontology

Deontological ethics

What makes an act right or wrong…

1 the **consequences** of the act *or*
2 something about the **nature of the act itself**, regardless *more or less* of the consequences?

The rather highfalutin term 'deontology' describes those ethical systems that adopt the second viewpoint. Deontological ethics is often described in opposition to **utilitarianism**, which adopts the consequentialist point of view (see Chapter 3).

Key term: deontology
The term deontology is derived from the Greek word *dei* meaning 'I must' and, of course, the suffix 'logy' meaning the 'the study of'.

Deontology is concerned with the rightness and wrongness of the act itself

In this chapter we will look at:

* **moral absolutism** and its relationship to deontology
* the ethical philosophy of **Immanuel Kant** and the **categorical imperative**
* some **criticisms** and **defences** of deontological ethics.

● 'You must, you must, you must…!'

Moral absolutism

Moral absolutism represents an extreme kind of deontological ethics. The moral absolutist will argue that an act is **intrinsically** right or wrong, **no matter** what the outcome and **whatever** the intentions.

For example, let's consider lying:

* a moral absolutist will insist that it is **always** wrong to lie, even if by lying you could, say, save a person's life
* other more **moderate deontologists** would argue that, while lying is wrong, in extreme circumstances where the consequences of not lying would be catastrophic, the wrong of lying *must* be committed
* a **utilitarian** might argue that lying is not right or wrong in itself, but becomes right or wrong according to the consequences of the lie.

What do you think of such absolute rules – do they help or hinder ethical judgements?

The Ten Commandments

Moral absolutism is often a stance adopted by **religion**, where deciding rightness and wrongness is ostensibly in the hands of a god, not human beings. Humans need only obey moral diktats, not reflect on ethical choices.

Perhaps the best-known code of absolutist ethics is the Decalogue, or **Ten Commandments** – various versions of which are found in Judaism and Christianity. These include injunctions such as:

- You shall not kill/murder. (Which depends on the translation!)
- You shall not commit adultery.
- You shall not steal.
- You shall not bear witness against your neighbour.

The Qur'an, too, includes a list of moral stipulations that can be related to the biblical Decalogue.

Kant and the categorical imperative

The ethical philosophers of the eighteenth century tried to place ethics on a purely rational basis. How, they wondered, can certain acts be shown to be intrinsically right or wrong in the light of **reason**, not just because custom or tradition has ordained such to be the case?

In answer, the German philosopher **Immanuel Kant** (1724–1804) developed the idea of the **categorical imperative**. In the *Groundwork of the Metaphysic of Morals* he divides the categorical imperative into **three formulations**, or maxims.

● Eighteenth-century philosophers placed reason at the forefront of their thought.

42

The First Formulation

Act only according to that maxim whereby you can at the same time will that it should become a universal law.

CASE STUDY: The Formula of the Universal Law

On what rational grounds would we accept the prohibition on stealing as a 'universal law'? Imagine a contrary ethical law – that stealing was a universal good. If stealing were the norm, then property could not exist and therefore stealing itself would be a nonsense. You would be faced with a kind of **ethical short circuit** and the law would have to be abandoned.

Try using the Formula of the Universal Law to show why lying would not pass Kant's test.

The Second Formulation

Act in such a way that you treat humanity, whether in your own person or in the person of any other, never merely as a means to an end, but always at the same time as an end.

Kant means that we should never treat others as *simply* tools or instruments in the pursuit of our own goals or desires. While we must all to some extent 'use' people in our daily interactions, we must always simultaneously recognize them as free, independent individuals – ('ends') like ourselves – and ensure that in some sense they have consented to being 'means'.

CASE STUDY: The Formula of the End in Itself

Slavery, of course, is an extreme example of the use of another human being as pure means. For Kant, enslaving another was a kind of philosophical act of bad faith. To deny another's freedom is tantamount to denying one's own.

The Third Formulation

Therefore, every rational being must so act as if he were through his maxim always a legislating member in the universal kingdom of ends.

For Kant, the 'kingdom of ends' is a kind of utopian vision of a society in which all the participants follow the first two formulations – free individuals who both make and obey rational universal laws.

● The kingdom of ends.

A passion*less* ethic?

Some thinkers have offered some very harsh criticisms of Kant's deontological ethics and no one more so than the later German philosopher **Friedrich Nietzsche** (1844–1900). Nietzsche thought Kant's ideas were little more than Christianity dressed up in secular clothes and especially disliked Kant's emphasis on a morality derived entirely from abstract, 'disembodied' reasoning:

'What could destroy us more quickly than working, thinking, and feeling without any inner necessity, without any deeply personal choice, without pleasure – as an automaton of "duty"? This is the very recipe for decadence, even for idiocy... Kant's Categorical Imperative endangered life itself.'

Friedrich Nietzsche, *The Antichrist*

Nonetheless deontology has survived such onslaughts and continues to find advocates among contemporary ethical thinkers. In its favour, they would probably argue:

* it provides a **general, rational basis** for making ethical decisions – we might not have to think through every moral dilemma in an effort to determine consequences; some actions we would already have recognized as indisputably wrong
* it draws a **clear line** for the extent of our moral responsibility – while we may be responsible for our acts we cannot be held responsible for their unforeseen consequences
* in its Kantian version at least, it empowers the agent as an ethical law maker in his or her own right.

5 Ethical concepts and values

Ethics in real life

So far in this book we have been looking at the major ethical theories or systems, as developed by moral philosophers. While such **overarching theories** are important in developing fresh perspectives on ethical thinking, they can sometimes seem remote from the real challenges faced by ordinary people in their personal and professional lives.

More than likely we will adopt a more **'syncretic'** (across-the-board) and **pragmatic approach**, making use of what we consider to be the best bits of virtue, utilitarian and deontological thought. **Values**, moreover, are more likely to sway us than theories.

In everyday life we adopt a pragmatic approach... values are more likely to sway us than theories

In the following chapters we'll be looking at **applied ethics** – how ethics can be applied to real situations. First of all, however, we'll tease out some of the key ethical concepts and values that keep cropping up in ethical debate:

* the related concepts of **freedom** and **responsibility** and how they underpin the possibility of moral choice making
* the concept of **'ethical values'** together with some key examples
* the **Golden Rule** – 'Do as you would be done by' – as a moral touchstone
* the concepts of **'natural rights'** and **'natural duties'**.

Freedom and responsibility

Limitations on human freedom are sometimes considered to be set by:

1 **relative determinism** – environment, upbringing and so on
2 **metaphysical determinism** – the idea that we are 'trapped' in a universe of cause and effect from which we cannot escape.

Freedom, however, is a crucial value in ethics. If human beings are not in some sense free, how can we ever be held responsible for our actions? Without freedom, there could be no wrong or right, good or evil, morally speaking, because no one could ever truly make a choice.

Ethical thinkers are therefore likely to accept that (1) may diminish our responsibility but deny (2) altogether, or at least suggest we should act as if it were not the case.

● If we did not enjoy some kind of freedom we would have as much responsibility for our action as someone on a roller-coaster is responsible for their direction of travel!

52

> **'A man who is convinced he possesses freedom of choice or free will has a greater sense of responsibility than a person who thinks that total determinism rules the universe and human life...'**
>
> Corliss Lamont, American philosopher, 1902–95

Existentialist freedom

The French existentialist philosophers such as **Jean-Paul Sartre** (1905–80) argued that freedom is at the very heart of what it means to be human. We alone have responsibility for our lives and this, Sartre believed, can be a terrifying **burden**. No wonder, he pointed out, so many people claim that they are a victim of circumstances or that their fate is in God's hands.

Values

Values are another key concept in ethics – if we can work out and agree what is **valuable** to us, then we can begin to choose those acts and rules that seem to nourish and conserve those values. In other words, values are the **ideals** or 'goods' that ethical action is built upon and aims at.

Some possible – and widely cherished – values include:

* **Equality** – According to this value, people who are similarly situated should be treated similarly – e.g. 'All children should receive a good education, regardless of economic status or class.'
* **Freedom** – Freedom, as we have seen, is fundamental to the possibility for ethical choice. However, it is also a common ethical goal – in the liberal, free-market West, actions, rules and laws that maximize and respect the liberty of the individual have become almost a supreme, 'umbrella' value.
* **Fraternity** (or **'community'**) – Actions should aim to foster the cohesion, mutuality and general friendliness of a group.

54

Two problems with values are immediately apparent:

1 Their exact meaning and even their absolute desirability are open to debate.
2 In certain situations, values may be in **competition** – for example, freedom and equality are often at loggerheads, especially in a free-market society. This, of course, does not necessarily undermine the validity of the value; only that some kind of ethical compromise must be reached.

'Liberté, egalité, fraternité!'
The rallying cry of the 1789 French Revolution

The Golden Rule: 'Do as you would be done by.'

This powerful, simple guide to right behaviour is also one of the most ancient and prevalent:

'Now this is the command: Do to the doer to cause that he do.'

The Eloquent Peasant, a story from the Middle Kingdom of ancient Egypt

'Here certainly is the golden maxim: Do not do to others that which we do not want them to do to us.'

Confucius

'Do unto others as you would have them do unto you.'

Gospel of Matthew

The Golden Rule offers a neat moral balance between **altruism** – the desire to act for others' sake – and **egoism** – the desire to act for one's own – and thus may well seem to be in tune with the realities of human nature. The simplicity of the ethic, however, is double-edged:

1 it has credibility across **all cultures** and times, *because of* the absence of relative moral values
2 the absence of any specific values (apart from reciprocity) can make it seem **meaningless** and trivial.

The Golden Rule is perhaps best thought of as a kind of **moral touchstone**, to be used in conjunction with more complex ethical thought.

● 'Well, you know I'd do the same thing for you!'

Rights and duties

Rights...

We can describe rights as a kind of 'good' that we are **entitled** to, rather than merely aspire to. We might well *want* to be rich, but we are *entitled* to liberty.

From an ethical point of view it is important to distinguish between:

1 **legal rights** – the rights given to citizens by laws, which are determined by a country's culture, traditions and ethos, *and*
2 **natural rights** – which are universal and inalienable.

For the English philosopher **John Locke** (1632–1704) natural rights could be summed up as 'life, liberty, and estate [property]'. Other philosophers have gone deeper, arguing that natural rights are bound up with human beings' very existence as **persons** – morally autonomous individuals whose innate freedom **cannot be surrendered or compromised** whatever the tyranny they live under. (We'll return to rights in Chapter 10.)

58

Duties...

Just as we can speak of natural rights, we can also speak of 'natural duties' – **universal duties** to which every human should be held. The US philosopher **John Rawls** (1921–2002) argued for the following natural duties:

* ✳ the duty not to be cruel
* ✳ the duty not to injure and the duty not to harm the innocent
* ✳ the duty to help one another
* ✳ the duty of justice
* ✳ the duty of mutual respect.

Natural rights and duties might be seen as providing a **comprehensive moral framework** for how the individual is to flourish as part of his or her community.

Natural rights and duties might be seen as providing a comprehensive moral framework for how the individual is to flourish as part of his or her community

6 A matter of life and death

Making moral judgements

For the ancient Greeks, as we have seen, the key question of moral philosophy was an eminently practical one – **how ought we to live?** Through the subsequent centuries, however, the close connection between moral philosophy and everyday life and lived experience was often lost beneath a concern for **meta-ethics** – for the abstract pondering on the meaning of right and wrong, of *how* we could make moral judgements in the first place.

After the devastation of World War II and the absolute horror of the Holocaust, there was a renewed engagement with **applied ethics** – the application of ethical systems such as deontology and utilitarianism to a host of pressing moral questions and issues.

Nowhere has this re-engagement been clearer than with respect to a cluster of issues focusing on the beginning and ending of human life.

In this chapter we will look at:

* some moral arguments for and against **capital punishment**
* the especially fraught issue of **abortion**
* what philosophers have said about **suicide**
* the issue of euthanasia, and in particular **voluntary active euthanasia**.

● 'What a quandary! Should I or shouldn't I have bought those shoes?'

Capital punishment

Capital punishment – the death penalty for crimes such as murder – has been abolished in many Western countries (with the notable exception of most of the United States). Nonetheless, research surveys repeatedly suggest that majorities would like to see it reintroduced, so it remains a **contentious ethical issue**.

Here are some of the ethical arguments both for and against capital punishment:

For...

* The argument from **justice** – for an ultimate crime such as murder, people deserve to suffer the ultimate penalty.
* The argument from **utility** – it acts as a deterrent, prevents the criminal from reoffending and satisfies the desire for revenge of relatives and so on.

64

Against...

* The **'one mistake'** argument – the mistaken execution of even one innocent person for a crime they did not commit makes capital punishment morally invalid.
* The **deontological** argument – if it is wrong to kill another human being, how can state-sanctioned killing be justified?
* The **responsibility** argument – the actions of human beings are always in some degree 'controlled' by circumstantial pressures such as upbringing; how therefore can we hold a murderer responsible for his or her actions?

Camus on the death penalty

In his 1957 essay *Reflections on the Guillotine*, the French philosopher **Albert Camus** (1913–1960) made a utilitarian case against capital punishment that the suffering inflicted on both the criminal as he awaits execution and his friends and family equalled or even outstripped the suffering of his victim and family (since the suffering is anticipated).

Abortion

Abortion – the termination of pregnancy – is an issue that causes a great deal of pain, anger and moral indignation on both sides of the moral argument…

1 those who support a woman's right to choose (the **'pro-choice'** camp) *and*
2 those who believe it is categorically wrong to end human life, even within the womb (the **'pro-life'** camp).

Even if we accept the primary argument of (1) – that of a woman's individual liberty to control her body and reproduction – this still leaves the central question unanswered: why should the foetus not be protected from harm like any other human being?

The ethical status of the foetus

We are all likely to accept the moral principle that it is wrong to kill an innocent human being. This, however, begs the question: when does a human being *become* a human being?:

* at **conception**, with the fertilized egg?
* at **birth**?
* with **viability**, when the child would be able to survive outside the womb, with, perhaps, medical assistance?
* or at some other point during foetal development?

We are all likely to be able to offer arguments for and against some of these possibilities. Viability, for example, is dependent on **medical technology**, which may be available in a Western context but unavailable elsewhere. Does, then, the ethical status of the foetus shift according to something as arbitrary as geography, too?

For this thorny reason of definition, abortion is likely to remain a fraught issue, **resistant to ethical compromise**.

Suicide

Suicide, usually taken to mean **intentional self-destruction**, is an issue that has preoccupied many philosophers, since it provides a particularly intense dramatization of a key ethical issue – to what extent should an individual be free to **choose his or her own destiny**, and what are the **claims of society and God**?

Look at the following philosophers' ideas and consider your own point of view:

'When a man's circumstances contain a preponderance of things in accordance with nature, it is appropriate for him to remain alive; when he possesses or sees in prospect a majority of the contrary things, it is appropriate for him to depart from life...'

Cicero

'The law [the Ten Commandments], rightly interpreted, even prohibits suicide, where it says, "Thou shalt not kill."'

St Augustine

'Every man is part of the community... and by killing himself he injures the community.'

St Thomas Aquinas

'...disposing of oneself as a mere means to some discretionary end is debasing humanity in one's person...'

Immanuel Kant

'We only arrive at ourselves in a freely chosen death.'

Jean Améry

Euthanasia

In recent years, ethical debate on euthanasia has focused on whether the state should or should not sanction arrangements where a doctor or some other person helps an individual suffering from a terminal or unbearable medical condition to die. This is called **voluntary active euthanasia**.

Key term: euthanasia

Euthanasia – derived from the Greek for 'good death' – is usually divided into active and passive kinds. **Active** euthanasia occurs where someone kills another painlessly to prevent suffering; **passive** euthanasia is where the death is intentionally not prevented (e.g. by medical intervention).

While we may defend the right of a person to commit suicide, can we ever condone someone who takes it upon him or herself to kill another person, even in that person's interest and with their full consent?

For...

✳ The **utilitarian** argument – if we have a duty to help those who are suffering, why should that duty not include an obligation to help them to end their suffering altogether, where there are no other means to allay it?

✳ The **libertarian** argument – if an individual has a right to refuse medical treatment that could save his or her life, he or she also has a right to demand medical assistance to end it.

Against...

✳ The **'Hippocratic' constraint** – doctors are bound by their professional code of ethics not to kill or harm their patients.

✳ The **'slippery slope' argument** – the sanctioning of voluntary active euthanasia could lead to cases of abuse; for example, the 'consent' of the patient may be given under duress.

7 Poverty, sex, war...

Hard decisions

As I have been at pains to emphasize, ethics is not – or is only very rarely – a cut-and-dried exercise. In its applied form, it must deal with the real world and with real situations, and as such it must be prepared to evolve and respond flexibly to the endless array of **competing interests** and **subtle ambiguities** that real life can throw at us.

In this sense, ethics is about equipping ourselves with the tools to think through difficult, challenging issues clearly and productively, and then acting accordingly. It is not about producing ready-made solutions out of the bag and it is certainly not about being 'high and mighty'.

If all this sounds like hard work – well, it is!

Ethics is about equipping ourselves with the tools to think through difficult, challenging issues clearly and productively

In this chapter we will examine some big issues and how ethics can help us to address them. We'll look at:

* **poverty** – what is the extent of our duty to alleviate others' poverty?
* **sex** – what role should ethics play in governing sexuality?
* **war** – when is it right to go to war?

● Ethics can seem like a lot of hard work... but it helps to have the right tools!

Poverty

In 1971 the Australian utilitarian philosopher **Peter Singer** (1946–) published an influential essay entitled 'Famine, Affluence and Morality' in which he made a powerful attack on the moral shortcomings of affluent Western citizens and laid down strict parameters for the extent of our duties. He made the following argument:

1 Poverty is bad – it causes **suffering**.
2 If we can prevent suffering we have a duty to do so, if in so doing we do not need to make any sacrifices of **comparable moral worth** (i.e. we need not plunge ourselves into poverty to save others from poverty).
3 Suffering is suffering whether it is **near or far away** – whether the poverty occurs in our own country or on the other side of the planet is irrelevant, ethically speaking.

On these grounds, Singer argued that generally people in the West should give a great deal more of their income to tackling **global poverty** than is currently the norm. When we are tempted to buy a new shirt or pair of shoes for the sake of fashion or vanity (and not because we need them), he insisted that we should give the money to an anti-poverty charity instead.

Singer's ethical command is demanding and for this reason has been criticized as unrealistic. Nonetheless, it remains a powerful moral battle cry in the struggle to combat global poverty.

● 'Well, I really do *need* another of those diamond-encrusted handbags, darling… and I just won't be happy till I get it!'

Sex

* Sex is an area of human activity where 'moralists' – though perhaps not ethicists – have only been too eager to lay down the law. Traditionally, sexual morality has often been viewed from an **absolutist**, puritanical point of view: thus homosexuality, premarital or extramarital sex, etc., are always wrong *in themselves*.

* In the second half of the twentieth century, however – at least in the secular, liberal West – sex and ethics embarked on a new relationship that is probably best characterized as **utilitarian**: there is no need for either society or state to interfere in people's sex lives unless that sex is considered in some sense to be a **harm**.

● Ethics even penetrate to our most intimate and private relations.

Modern sexual ethics is thus concerned with what constitutes a harm in sexual activity and typically focuses on the following core issues:

1 **Informed consent** – participants must freely and fully consent to sexual activity. While this self-evidently excludes a clear breach of consent as in the case of sex with children or rape, there are many ethically 'grey' areas, e.g. sex under the influence of alcohol or drugs.

2 **Abuse of power** – sexual activity between participants where there is an unequal power relation (e.g. between adult and juvenile, doctor and patient, teacher and student) is usually considered unethical, in part because such inequality erodes the viability of consent.

3 **Actual harm** – the inflicting of actual harm during sex, e.g. where a participant engages in unprotected sex knowing he or she may transmit HIV.

Sexual ethics – two case studies

Pornography

The proliferation of so-called 'Internet porn' in the last decade has intensified a long-standing debate over the ethical status of pornography. Can pornography – both in terms of its production and consumption – be construed as in any sense harmful, either to individuals or society more generally?

Here are some typical views:

It's a question of personal freedom!

It views humans purely as means and not ends and hence debases human sexuality.

It's a kind of 'speech' and as such should be protected!

It can act as a safety mechanism – diffusing potentially violent or abusive fantasies.

It's an abuse of the people involved – whether they have consented or not!

Prostitution

Prostitution involves the selling of sexual services for money – generally (but not at all exclusively) by women to men. Its ethical status is a matter of intense debate – a fact reflected in the varied legal regimes under which it operates in different countries around the world.

Below is a spider chart showing the **competing** ethical principles, values and issues that come into play:

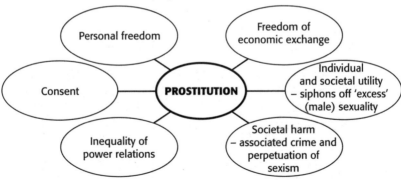

War

When is it right to go to war?

'For it is the injustice of the opposing side that lays on the wise man the duty of waging wars...'

St Augustine

For the Christian thinker St Augustine, war may be justified – despite the biblical prohibition on killing – where it is waged against a wrongdoer and therefore can be seen as a kind of **wholesale punishment**.

St Augustine's notion of the **'just war'** has had a powerful influence over Western civilization. We find echoes of it, for example, in the US and British justification of the invasion of Iraq in 2003, which was often cast in the light of a 'moral crusade' against an unjust dictator. The problem is, of course, that justice, like beauty, may be in the eye of the beholder.

Today war is often said to be justified where:

* it is in **self-defence**
* it is the **last resort**
* civilian **non-combatants** are not harmed
* a **successful outcome** is likely.

A survey of recent conflicts suggest that war can rarely, if ever, be as morally unambiguous as this. War is a messy, ugly business and stubbornly resists ethical posturings:

* is it ever possible to avoid civilian casualties, even in modern 'technological' warfare?
* are combatants really less worthy of protection than civilians?

8 Animals and the environment

Ethics and the wider world

Traditional ethics concerned itself largely with **interpersonal relationships** – how, it asked, should we treat our fellow human beings? In the twentieth and twenty-first centuries – in the face of rapid environmental change and the threat of ecological catastrophe – ethical thinking has been extended and deepened to encompass humans' relationship to the world around them.

* What are our **duties** to animals, as sentient beings?
* What our duties to the very land itself?
* Can we really speak of non-human subjects – a forest, an ecosystem – as having **rights**?

What are man's duties to animals and to the very land itself?

In this chapter we will look at:

* the development of animal rights and the concept of **speciesism**
* **environmental ethics**
* a case study about **wildernesses** and why we might want to conserve them.

● 'We don't have to run this race, you know. We do have rights!'

The traditional perspective

Traditionally animals were considered to have **no ethical status**; it was even denied that they need be a matter of ethical concern at all. Such views usually depended on some sense that animals **lacked feelings**:

* the French philosopher René Descartes thought that animals were simply **machines** without any consciousness
* Kant argued that, since animals were not rational, they could not be said to be 'ends in themselves' like human beings and therefore had no moral status or **rights**.

Such views turned animals into little more than tools for mankind's wellbeing and advancement – as a source of food and clothing, beasts of burden, or subjects for experimentation (vivisection).

Where animals did have some ethical value was as the **subjects of human virtue**. Kant, for example, believed that showing kindness to animals was simply good practice for showing kindness to other humans:

'We can judge the heart of a man by his treatment of animals.'

Touching as this may sound, it left animals in a kind of ethical vacuum, their wellbeing dependent on the whim of their human 'superiors'.

Jeremy Bentham was the first important philosopher to accord animals **rights for their own sake**:

'...the question is not, Can they reason? nor, Can they talk? but, Can they suffer? Why should the law refuse its protection to any sensitive being? ...the time will come when humanity will extend its mantle over everything which breathes...'

Animal rights... and wrongs

The ethically **anthropocentric** view of animals – subjects of either human cruelty or kindness – was increasingly challenged in the twentieth century.

Some philosophers – notably Peter Singer – argued that animals, as sentient beings, have **equal interests** to humans and that their interests must be taken fully into account. To deny them this amounts to **speciesism**.

Singer thus made the following (some might say extreme) arguments:

* **vegetarianism** is the only ethical diet since human pleasure in eating meat can never ethically outweigh the suffering of animals bred to supply it
* **animal experimentation** can only be defended if we believe that it would also be right to experiment on an orphaned child with a mental capacity similar to a 'non-human animal'.

Subjects-of-a-life

Another philosopher, the American **Tom Regan** (1938–), insists that animals have rights, not because of their ability to suffer (the utilitarian point of view), but because they have **inherent value** as what he calls 'subjects-of-a-life'.

Following Singer's point of view, suffering inflicted on an animal might be justified where a greater interest is served. In Regan's view, such suffering is **never** justifiable.

Both Singer's and Regan's views had a powerful political impact on the animal 'liberation' and welfare movements of the 1970s and beyond. They also undeniably helped inform:

* the (relatively) more humane approaches to farming adopted in many Western countries today *as well as*
* the much stricter ethical governance of animal experimentation.

Environmental ethics

In the twentieth century and beyond thinkers have sought to extend the reach of ethical rights and duties outside the human community and into the **natural environment**. They have asked specific ethical questions such as:

* can we justify cutting down the planet's rainforests for the sake of human industry and jobs?
* do we have a duty to try and preserve a species from extinction?
* should a wilderness like Antarctica be open to exploitation?

Often thinkers have used traditional ethical theories such as utilitarianism and deontology to help resolve such issues, weighing up the competing interests so as to come up with some kind of **compromise**.

Some environmental ethicists, however, have called for a whole **new ethics**.

92

Towards a new ethics

Conventional philosophy, they argue, has tended to view human beings as different from, and superior, to their environment. Any ethics rooted in this standpoint – such as utilitarianism – is therefore anthropocentric in its nature, giving human beings carte blanche to exploit the environment ruthlessly for their short-term gain.

'Deep ecologists' argue that humans and all other life forms are part of one holistic system and that a truly environmental ethics needs to recognize this. Thus they might argue:

* a forest (or any other ecosystem) has an **inalienable right** to exist
* the genetic survival of a **species** is of greater importance than the survival of any individual life form
* the future survival of the natural environment **as a whole** must be the primary ethical value and goal.

The future survival of the natural environment as a whole must be the primary ethical value and goal

Conserving the wilderness

Today the Earth has very little true wilderness – that is, environments left (as far as is possible) unchanged by human habitation or enterprise; in the United States, for example, only about five per cent of the landscape is so categorized and protected by law. We may instinctively wish to preserve such wildernesses, but on what ethical grounds should we protect or conserve them?

Conventional utilitarian ethics would offer wildernesses **no real protection** since they have no real utility except perhaps as glorified recreational parks – places for 'hunting, shooting and fishing' or perhaps spiritual contemplation. Any competing human interest would soon trump such a feeble basis for conservation.

● On what ethical grounds should we conserve nature?

94

Environmental ethicists argue that wildernesses have an intrinsic value in their own right. As early as the 1920s the American ecologist **Aldo Leopold** (1887–1948) – later founder of the Wilderness Society – argued such landscapes should be maintained as near to a state of nature as possible and not in any way viewed as objects for human domination, conquest or recreation.

For Leopold, this ethic – based not on human self-interest but on a net of empathy and responsibility thrown as wide as possible – connected the conservation of wildernesses with our day-to-day treatment of our fellow man:

> ## 'Of what avail are forty freedoms without a blank spot on the map?'

9 Professional ethics

Ethics and codes of conduct

Professional ethics in the form of ethical codes of conduct have existed since ancient times. Perhaps the oldest is the so-called **Hippocratic Oath** (5th century BCE) dealing with the proper relations between doctors and their patients and which continues to exist (in modified form) to this day.

In modern times professional codes of conduct have proliferated – lawyers, business owners, social workers and many other professionals, as well as doctors and other health practitioners, are obliged to follow a set of strict moral principles. **Beneficence** – acting in the client's or patient's interest – is a universal and perhaps primary professional value.

While such codes do not have the force of law, failure to adhere to them can lead to the individual being expelled from the professional body and thus barred from practice.

As in every other field of applied ethics, professionals may be faced with **ethical dilemmas** that result from competing or contradictory values.

In this chapter we will look at:

* **business** ethics
* **medical** ethics and the related field of biomedical research
* **legal** ethics.

● 'Well, you're safe in my hands… I've sworn an oath to protect you!'

Business ethics

Is the sole concern of business merely **to maximize profit**? Some have argued with a categorical 'yes' and deny that business – both the individuals working in business and the corporations to which they belong – have any other ethical duties other than those to which they are constrained by the law. Making money, in this view, is the ethic, pure and simple:

'Greed, for lack of a better word, is good.'

'Gordon Gecko', *Wall Street* (1987)

Since the 1980s, nonetheless, business ethics has become an important discipline. The sheer power and reach of global corporations, the increasing demand for transparency, and a concern with good public relations not necessarily synonymous with 'window-dressing', have led companies (and those who regulate them) to pay closer attention to how they behave. The global banking crisis of 2008–9 was a dramatic illustration of the limits and limitations of current notions of 'corporate responsibility'.

Business ethics typically concerns itself with the following questions (among others):

* What are the duties of business towards **workers**? (e.g. union rights)
* What are its duties towards **customers**? (e.g. product safety)
* What are its responsibilities to **society** in general? (e.g. protecting the environment)
* What are the responsibilities of international corporations towards less developed countries? (e.g. child labour)
* How can a company be structured so that unethical behaviour is discouraged and ethical behaviour encouraged?

● 'To improve our company profile, I've decided that, going forward, all managers will be voluntarily donating 20 per cent of their salaries to the Dolphin Fund. Thoughts, anyone?'

Medical ethics

Doctors, nurses and other health practitioners are often faced with complex ethical dilemmas. An understanding of the **core values** of medical ethics can help them to resolve such cases:

JUSTICE
Medical treatment must be distributed fairly among patients

BENEFICENCE
The primary goal of the practitioner is the welfare of the patient

HONESTY
The patient has the right to be fully informed about their medical condition and any proposed treatment

MEDICAL DECISION

AUTONOMY
The patient has the right to accept or refuse treatment

NON-MALEFICENCE
The practitioner must not harm the patient

CASE STUDY: Medical dilemmas

Such core values may quite often come into conflict – for example:

* **Beneficence versus autonomy** – a patient refuses treatment that a doctor knows will save their life.
* **Beneficence versus non-maleficence** – palliative drugs administered towards the end of a patient's life may simultaneously hasten death.
* **Honesty versus non-maleficence** – telling the patient the full facts about their condition may cause them psychological harm.
* **Beneficence versus justice** – scarce resources may lead a doctor to decide to treat one patient in preference to another.

Rather than applying ethical principles wholesale, medical practitioners generally prefer responding sensitively on a **case-by-case basis**.

Bioethics

Bioethics concerns itself with the ethical issues relating to developments in the **biological sciences**. Debates highlighted in recent years have included:

* **Genetic engineering** of crops and animals:
  » Are genetically modified crops any different, ethically speaking, from traditional breeding programmes?
  » Is there something wrong with such interference with 'nature' when we do not really know the consequences?
* **Genetic testing** of the human foetus for medical conditions:
  » Is it wrong to abort a foetus in order to prevent the birth of a child with a potentially devastating condition or disability?
  » Does a doctor have a duty of care to prevent such *potential* suffering?

Like related issues such as abortion, such questions can become highly emotive and inflamed.

104

CASE STUDY: Embryonic stem cell research

Stem cells are 'general' biological cells that can self-renew and which can develop into any of the specialized cells that make up human tissue. Research suggests that stem cells have massive potential to treat medical conditions such as degenerative diseases and genetic disorders.

Despite the huge potential benefits, the creation and exploitation of embryonic stem cells have unleashed a fierce ethical debate:

* 'pro-lifers' argue, on the **sanctity of life** principle, that the exploitation of human embryos, however they are produced, is tantamount to murder
* supporters of embryonic stem cell research argue that, in the very earliest days of their development (up to 14 days), embryos have **no capacity to feel pain** and as such have, as yet, no status as a person entitled to protection.

Legal ethics

Lawyers and other legal practitioners are usually governed by a professional code of conduct in order to protect clients and to maintain the **integrity of the legal system**. In the United Kingdom, for example, solicitors are bound by the Solicitors' Code of Conduct 2007, while in the United States attorneys generally follow a version of the American Bar Association's model rules.

Such codes focus on a range of issues including:

* **conflict of interest** – typically a lawyer should not act for two clients where furthering the interests of one is detrimental to the interests of the other
* **lawyer–client confidentiality** – lawyers should not disclose information imparted to them by clients except with the latter's permission
* **dual responsibility** – even while they pursue the interests of private clients, lawyers simultaneously have a public duty to ensure that justice is fairly administered

Lawyers and other legal practitioners are usually governed by a professional code of conduct in order to protect clients and to maintain the integrity of the legal system

* **fees** – fees should be fair and reasonable
* **advertising** – traditionally lawyers were barred from advertising their services; this rule has been relaxed in some countries such as the UK and USA.

● In many professions, confidentiality is a core ethical value, serving to foster trust and honesty between practitioner and client.

10 Ethics and the law

Good laws, bad laws

We might expect that laws would have a strong ethical quality. The earliest known legal code – the Sumerian Code of Ur-Nammu (c. 2100 BCE) – sought **'equity** in the land' – something we'd recognize as a prime ethical and legal value today (even though some of what the Code considered criminal would not be deemed so today).

History shows us, however, that there have been plenty of societies in which the laws have been flagrantly **immoral**. While the anti-Semitic laws introduced by Germany in the 1930s undoubtedly reflected the *ethos* of the Nazi regime, they flew in the face of all established *ethics*.

What is the proper relationship between ethics and law?

The problem is that laws, of course, are often created by **imperfect rulers** or can grow up rather **haphazardly** over time. In this way, law and ethics can easily part company.

In this chapter we will look at:

* some different ideas about how ethics and law should relate to one another *and*
* the Universal Declaration of Human Rights – which many would consider to be a supreme expression of ethics as law.

Morality in relation to the law

There are three main strands of thought about what the proper relationship between morality and law should be:

1 there is **no direct relationship** – law is simply what is established by authority and often sanctioned by tradition
2 the making of laws should directly relate to **abstract ethical reasoning**
3 laws are made by a **combination of (1) and (2)**, evolving as established laws are assessed and reinterpreted in the light of the values of the day.

The third solution is that adopted in Western societies today, since it roots the law in firm ground and yet allows for its organic growth as society's ethical consciousness itself evolves, expands and deepens. Changes in law – for example, with regard to voluntary assisted suicide or genetic research – will ideally follow (or will not follow) after **sustained ethical debate**.

112

Natural law

Another way of looking at the relationship between ethics and law is through the prism of natural law. In Chapter 5 we looked at the distinction between:

1 **legal rights** – the rights given to citizens by laws, which are determined by a country's culture, traditions and ethos, *and*
2 **natural rights** – which are universal and inalienable.

Once again, we might ideally expect, or hope, that legal rights would evolve towards a closer reflection of natural rights (while not, perhaps, losing sight of their origins).

Nevertheless, the relationship between the two can sometimes be fraught, as shown in the UK, for example, in the tension between home-grown laws and the European Convention on Human Rights (incorporated into UK law as the Human Rights Act 1998), particularly over such issues as privacy and the rights of offenders.

The Universal Declaration of Human Rights

In 1948 the United Nations issued the Universal Declaration of Human Rights (UDHR), whose 30 articles lay out the **fundamental rights of all human beings**. Since 1976 the UDHR has had the status of international law and, while it has attracted some criticism (principally on cultural and religious grounds), is thus currently the most ambitious attempt to realize natural rights in a legal format.

'We stand today at the threshold of a great event both in the life of the United Nations and in the life of mankind. This declaration may well become the international Magna Carta for all men everywhere.'

Eleanor Roosevelt, in a speech given to the UN General Assembly on the adoption of the Universal Declaration

The articles (with some abbreviation) are:

1 *All human beings are born free and equal in dignity and rights…*
2 *Everyone is entitled to all the rights and freedoms set forth in this Declaration, without distinction of any kind, such as race, colour, sex, language, religion, political or other opinion, national or social origin, property, birth or other status…*
3 *Everyone has the right to life, liberty and security of person.*
4 *No one shall be held in slavery or servitude…*
5 *No one shall be subjected to torture or to cruel, inhuman or degrading treatment or punishment.*
6 *Everyone has the right to recognition everywhere as a person before the law.*
7 *All are equal before the law and are entitled without any discrimination to equal protection of the law…*
8 *Everyone has the right to an effective remedy by the competent national tribunals for acts violating the fundamental rights granted him by the constitution or by law.*

The Universal Declaration of Human Rights

9 *No one shall be subjected to arbitrary arrest, detention or exile.*

10 *Everyone is entitled in full equality to a fair and public hearing by an independent and impartial tribunal...*

11 *Everyone charged with a penal offence has the right to be presumed innocent until proved guilty...*

12 *No one shall be subjected to arbitrary interference with his privacy, family, home or correspondence, nor to attacks upon his honour and reputation.*

13 *Everyone has the right to freedom of movement and residence within the borders of each state...*

14 *Everyone has the right to seek and to enjoy in other countries asylum from persecution...*

15 *Everyone has the right to a nationality...*

16 *Men and women of full age, without any limitation due to race, nationality or religion, have the right to marry and to found a family...*

17 *Everyone has the right to own property alone as well as in association with others...*
18 *Everyone has the right to freedom of thought, conscience and religion...*

● The freedom of movement.

The Universal Declaration of Human Rights

19 *Everyone has the right to freedom of opinion and expression...*

20 *Everyone has the right to freedom of peaceful assembly and association...*

21 *Everyone has the right to take part in the government of his country, directly or through freely chosen representatives...*

22 *Everyone, as a member of society, has the right to social security and is entitled to realization... of the economic, social and cultural rights indispensable for his dignity and the free development of his personality.*

23 *Everyone has the right to work, to free choice of employment, to just and favourable conditions of work and to protection against unemployment...*

24 *Everyone has the right to rest and leisure...*

25 *Everyone has the right to a standard of living adequate for the health and wellbeing of himself and of his family...*

26 *Everyone has the right to education...*

27 *Everyone has the right freely to participate in the cultural life of the community…*

28 *Everyone is entitled to a social and international order in which the rights and freedoms set forth in this Declaration can be fully realized.*

29 *Everyone has duties to the community in which alone the free and full development of his personality is possible…*

30 *Nothing in this Declaration may be interpreted as implying for any State, group or person any right to engage in any activity or to perform any act aimed at the destruction of any of the rights and freedoms set forth herein.*

● The freedom of expression.

Further reading

Perhaps as a **starting point** you could do no better than Simon Blackburn's brilliantly lucid *Being Good: A Short Introduction to Ethics* (Oxford, 2002). Short and compact it may be, but it is bursting with ideas.

Turning to the principal ethical theories covered in this book, Aristotle's *Nicomachean Ethics* (Penguin, 2004) is, of course, the foundational text of **virtue ethics** and a surprisingly good read. For **utilitarianism**, Bentham's own writings are perhaps a challenge too far; better to turn to his Victorian follower John Stuart Mill and the collection *On Liberty and Other Essays* (Oxford World Classics, 2008). Kant, too, is a daunting prospect, so for an examination of his approach to **deontology** it might be best to reach for Paul Guyer's *Kant* (Routledge, 2006), part of The Routledge Philosophers series.

In terms of **applied ethics**, I would recommend choosing one of the many compendia of essays that are available – *A Companion to Applied Ethics* (2005) edited by R. G. Frey and Christopher Heath Wellman is an excellent example.